The
Ten Second
Message

Compiled by

Dan McKinnon

House of Hits
New York

The Ten Second Message

Copyright © 1994

by
House of Hits Publishing
Building 75
JFK International Airport
Jamaica, NY 11430

Library of Congress Cataloging-In-Publication Data
ISBN 0-941437-04-3
Library of Congress Card Number: 94-77357

The Ten Second Message
Compiled by
Dan McKinnon

Printed in the United States of America
7 6 5 4 3 2 1

Index

Thanks, Mom
for
planting the
seeds.

Introduction

Often a preacher capsulizes his message in a few brief words.

Many times those expressions are so powerful they excite us in a way we never want to lose the thoughts. That's why many scribble such comments in the margins or on the back blank pages of their Bible.

These are a collection of those special phrases that in Ten Seconds or less convey awesome messages. They are from a variety of preachers I've been fortunate enough to hear over the years.

Hope you enjoy the feast.

— Dan McKinnon

With man
familiarity breeds contempt,

With God
familiarity breeds love.

God said what
He meant

and

He meant what
He said.

Ten Second Message

No God
No Peace

Know God
Know Peace

The closer
we get to God

The more we are aware
of
our sin.

God
pulls no surprises.

He
tells us exactly
what
to expect.

5

God promised
to deliver us

through
our trials

not

from them.

We had

an

unbeatable combination

God had the strength

and

I had the weakness.

7

You
can't walk with
the Lord
and
run with the Devil.

— S.M. Lockridge

God doesn't give
you a gift
because you want
or seek it.

God gives you the gift
He
wants you to have!

9

God
can do anything

but

maybe He doesn't
want
to do everything.

Ten Second Message

God is never late!

He's

always on time.

God
doesn't Love
some Christians
more than others

He

just enjoys
some Christians more
than others.

God

never

breaks anyone with

success

but

with: — heartache

— loneliness

— and pain.

13

If God believed
in permissiveness
He
would have given us
The
Ten Suggestions.

When you work for
God
the payment may not be
much
but
the retirement benefits
are
out of this world.

God
doesn't make
faulty products.

It takes more Faith
to believe
the world just happened

than that
God created it.

Those who serve
the best
get closest to the Power

whether its

The Boss
The President
or
God

Ten Second Message

To
Expect great things
from God

Attempt great things
for God.

— Hudson Taylor

This book
is either the
cornerstone of life

or a

stumbling block.

This book

will

keep you from sin

or

sin will keep you

from this book.

— John Bunyan

If
a man's Bible
is
coming apart

it is an indication
he himself
is pretty well put together.

If we're not
straight
about the Bible

we'll be
crooked
in everything else.

If
there were any
defects
in the Bible

who's
smart enought
to
detect them?

— S. M. Lockridge

Use of the Bible
doesn't give you
creditability

unless

you give the
Bible
creditability.

The Holy Spirit
and
the wind
are the same

you never see them
but
you see the effect.

Ten Second Message

Be careful
how you live

you
may be the only
Bible

some people read.

People do not
reject the Bible
because
it contradicts itself

but

because it
contradicts them.

Find help fast
in
the Bible pages.

It's not how you've
been through the
Bible

but how the Bible
has been through
you.

The Bible says it!

I believe it!

That settles it!

Nobody goes to
Hell
because they're a sinner

— but because they
reject
the solution to being
a sinner.

Ten Second Message

There are some
incurable diseases

but

sin isn't one of them.

Confessing
is agreeing with God

"I'm doing wrong."

The

wages of sin

will be paid.

When you become a
Christian

it doesn't mean you can't sin
but
you won't enjoy it.

It
wasn't the apple
on the tree that
got man in trouble

it was
the pair underneath.

Ten Second Message

God doesn't carry
a grudge

if

we confess our sins.

The advantage
of believing God's Word

is

we don't have to learn
the hard way
the destructive results
of sin.

The closer we

get to

God

the more

we are aware

of

our sin.

Inflation hasn't
affected the
wages of sin —

— It's still death.

Every physical disaster
has symptoms

Every spiritual disaster
has symptoms.

No other religion
of the world
deals with sin

only Christianity

that's why others
don't work.

Purpose of life

To tell others

about

Jesus.

Physical hunger —
the more you eat,
the less you want.

Spiritual hunger —
the more you eat,
the more you want.

45

How To Tell A Christian:

1. Zeal for personal purity.

2. Zeal to oppose unrighteousness.

3. Zeal for the Lord and to share Him with others.

~

— Lon Solomon

Ten Second Message

The

most certain fact of life

is

you will die

the

most uncertain fact

is

when.

Ten Second Message

John
wrote scripture
in the key of B

... Be saved.

No tomorrow
in the Bible
concerning salvation.

It's always today.

There may be no
tomorrow.

— Billy Graham

Never seen anyone

come to Christ

and regretted it

but

seen many who

refused

and were miserable.

— Billy Graham

Other Religions
reject
the creator

and

and worship creation.

Every Christian
has
three degrees:

B.A. Born Again
M.A. Mightily Altered
D.D. Divinely Destined

Ten Second Message

If you wish
to dwell in the house
of the
Lord

You must make your
reservation
in advance.

Accepting the Lord

is

more than a fire insurance

policy

it's

a way of life.

God didn't say
"Show me, then I'll
believe
but believe me,
then I'll show you."

— Billy Graham

All
religions of the world
have legalism:

live right, do right
and you'll be saved.

Only

Christianity has Grace.

He isn't the most
important thing in
your life

until

He
is the only thing.

57

If you asked Jesus
his age,
on his Mothers side
he'd say
"12 years old"

and
"On my Father's side
from
everlasting to everlasting."

~

— S.M. Lockridge

You never find
Jesus
is all you need

till

Jesus is all you've got.

59

Let the

Son

shine in.

If
you copy other peoples
lives

you copy their faults,

if you copy Jesus

there is no fault.

61

Jesus never argued
with the Devil,

Just answered him
with
the scriptures.

He may not

come

when you want Him

but

He always comes

on time.

— S.M. Lockridge

Angels rolled
away the stone

— not to let Jesus out
— but to let
the disciples in.

Prosecutors couldn't find
real fault with Jesus.
The only
accusation against Him
at His trial
was

blasphemy

not
lying,
cheating,
stealing...
but claiming to be God.

Which was truth!

There are several people
for whom I'd
give my life

but

there is no one
for whom
I'd give my son's life.

What a sacrifice by God!

Many
great men of God
have great weaknesses

but God honored
them

because they honored God
inspite of their weaknesses.

Lord lead
Lord guide
and
We'll be satisfied

— S.M. Lockridge

Seven Days

without

Prayer

Makes

one weak.

The only thing
God wants from
you

is

you!

Jesus loves you

whether

you're loveable

or

not.

~

He feared God
so much

he never dared

to
fear any man.

Giving
in a Church
is
never a money problem

it's

a heart problem.

God afflicts us
with people
according
to our needs.

Faith
is when I depend
on God,

Commitment
is when God can
depend on
me.

Look for the fruit

and

you'll uncover the root.

Jesus
cleaned me up
on the inside
and
gave me incentive
to
clean myself up on the
outside.

77

If your talk is all right

but

your walk all wrong,

Are you a Christian?

Witness
isn't something you do

it's
something you are.

A

Christian

is

only as powerful

as

he is pure.

Beware
of a leader who:

1. Doesn't respect authority.

2. Downplays purity.

3. Promises more than
God promises.

4. Rejects his Christian
experience.

Billy Graham
urges new converts

to:

Pray
Read the Bible
Witness
Go To Church.

God's reputation

is

largely determined

by

the way his

children act.

"I have everything
to live with...

But nothing to
live for."

You can come
Just as I am,

but God doesn't
plan for you to stay

Just as I am.

You're

either

a

missionary

or

mission field.

~

Not walkin'
His talk

~

If
you were on trial
for being a Christian,

would there be
enough evidence
to
convict you?

Many peoples concept
of Jesus
He is like the
Lone Ranger

that

"He just stands around
till we need
Him."

89

It doesn't take
much of a man
to be a
Christian

It takes all of him.

The secret
to walking with God

is to

keep the Main Thing,
the Main Thing.

— Ken Poure

91

"The most impressive thing about life,

It's so short"

— Billy Graham

We're all teminal cases

only

with different dates.

If we'd had welfare,
the prodigal son never
would have come home.

Dad was anxious to help
— but didn't until
changes in his son's heart.

When
there is the greatest pressure
to keep quiet,

and you speak up
as a Christian,

then your words will
carry
the geatest impact.

Five characteristics
of
false prophets:

1. Deny the truth of the Word of God,

2. Divide the Church,

3. Desire for money and power,

4. Indulge in immoral behavior,

5. Destroy peoples faith.

— Peter McKnight

Live as though
it were your last
day on Earth

Someday
you will be right.

Ten Second Message

God

Does not send men to

Hell

they chose it!

What do you need
to do
to go to Hell?

By doing nothing

you've done all
that's necessary.

Hell was not
made for man

It was made for the Devil
and his Angels

Man who rejects
God
just also goes there.

I'd rather spend
a little time
with a few hypocrites
in Church

than

spend eternity with
all
the hypocrites.

Don't
wring your hands
in despair

but

fold your hands
in prayer.

I've got everlasting life
when I die

I'm just
going to change locations.

Purpose of life
is
to tell others about
the
life saving power
of
Jesus.

He who is born
of God

should grow

to
resemble his Father.

105

Be a minuteman for
Christ

Always ready to
share the message.

Thermometer
reports temperature
of the room

Thermostat
sets the temperature
of the room.

Which do you do
for
Jesus Christ?

107

Nobody
can teach you
how
to be a Christian,

You learn it
on the job!

Ten Second Message

Following Christ
can be
condensed
into four words:

admit
submit
commit
transmit.

—Samuel Wilberforce

Thank God
for your condition

because
without God

you wouldn't have
any condition.

Ten Second Message

God
didn't love you
because
you're valuable

you're valuable
because
God loves you.

God
never lets us get
so old

that we
don't have to trust
Him

for something.

Ten Second Message

Problems
will make you

bitter or better.

~

Lost opportunities

for God

often

never come back.

Purpose of preaching
is to
constantly
remind mankind

of

what mankind
is
constantly forgetting.

Insurance
carries you to the grave

Assurance
carries you through eternity.

It doesn't matter
what happens to me

you're
going to get
what's
coming to you.

117

The
only thing
we can take to
Heaven
with us after death

is
family and friends
through faith
in
Jesus Christ.

Be sure you know
the uppertaker

before
you see
the
undertaker.

Why Church training
is so very important! —

"He who converts a soul,
draws water from a fountain;
but he who trains a
soulwinner,
digs a well
from which thousands
may drink eternal life..."

~

— Spurgeon

G = God

O = Offers

S = Sinful

P = People

E = Eternal

L = Life

Ten Second Message

To get into Heaven...

It's not what
you know

It's not what
you do

— but who you
know!

There are

NO
VISITORS

in Heaven.

Before
you cross
to the other side

be sure
you can do it
with pride.

Rapture

not here the day after
gone the day before

caught up
not burned up.

— S.M. Lockridge

Christians

have more fun

especially

later!

Notes

Notes